The Illustrated Poems of

# John Betjeman

# The Illustrated Poems of
# John Betjeman

## With Watercolours by
## David Gentleman

John Murray
*Albemarle Street, London*

First published in 1995
by John Murray (Publishers) Ltd,
50 Albemarle Street, London W1X 4BD

Reprinted 1998, 1999, 2002

Consultant: David Herbert. Designer: Pauline Harrison



A catalogue record for this book is available from the British Library

ISBN 0–7195–5248 6 (Hardback)
ISBN 0–7195–5532 9 (Paperback)
Typeset in Monotype (hot-metal) Garamond (156)
by Gloucester Typesetting Services, Stonehouse, Glos.
Printed and bound in Spain
by Bookprint, S.L., Barcelona

# CONTENTS

## LOVE

## CHURCH



## PEOPLE



## PLACES

DEATH

# LOVE

# Pot Pourri from a Surrey Garden

Miles of pram in the wind and Pam in the gorse track,
Coco-nut smell of the broom, and a packet of Weights
Press'd in the sand. The thud of a hoof on a horse-track –
A horse-riding horse for a horse-track –
Conifer county of Surrey approached
Through remarkable wrought-iron gates.

Over your boundary now, I wash my face in a bird-bath,
Then which path shall I take? that over there by the pram?
Down by the pond! or – yes, I will take the slippery third path,
Trodden away with gym shoes,
Beautiful fir-dry alley that leads
To the bountiful body of Pam.

Pam, I adore you, Pam, you great big mountainous sports girl,
Whizzing them over the net, full of the strength of five:
That old Malvernian brother, you zephyr and khaki shorts girl,
Although he's playing for Woking,
Can't stand up
To your wonderful backhand drive.

See the strength of her arm, as firm and hairy as Hendren's;
See the size of her thighs, the pout of her lips as, cross,
And full of a pent-up strength, she swipes at the rhododendrons,
Lucky the rhododendrons,
And flings her arrogant love-lock
Back with a petulant toss.

Over the redolent pinewoods, in at the bathroom casement,
One fine Saturday, Windlesham bells shall call:
Up the Butterfield aisle rich with Gothic enlacement,
Licensed now for embracement,
Pam and I, as the organ
Thunders over you all.

## Myfanwy

Kind o'er the *kinderbank* leans my Myfanwy,
White o'er the play-pen the sheen of her dress,
Fresh from the bathroom and soft in the nursery
Soap-scented fingers I long to caress.

Were you a prefect and head of your dormit'ry?
Were you a hockey girl, tennis or gym?
Who was your favourite? Who had a crush on you?
Which were the baths where they taught you to swim?

Smooth down the Avenue glitters the bicycle,
Black-stockinged legs under navy-blue serge,
Home and Colonial, Star, International,
Balancing bicycle leant on the verge.

Trace me your wheel-tracks, you fortunate bicycle,
Out of the shopping and into the dark,
Back down the Avenue, back to the pottingshed,
Back to the house on the fringe of the park.

Golden the light on the locks of Myfanwy,
Golden the light on the book on her knee,
Finger-marked pages of Rackham's Hans Andersen,
Time for the children to come down to tea.

Oh! Fuller's angel-cake, Robertson's marmalade,
Liberty lampshade, come, shine on us all,
My! what a spread for the friends of Myfanwy
Some in the alcove and some in the hall.

Then what sardines in the half-lighted passages!
Locking of fingers in long hide-and-seek.
You will protect me, my silken Myfanwy,
Ringleader, tom-boy, and chum to the weak.

## Myfanwy at Oxford

Pink may, double may, dead laburnum
   Shedding an Anglo-Jackson shade,
Shall we ever, my staunch Myfanwy,
   Bicycle down to North Parade?
Kant on the handle-bars, Marx in the saddlebag,
   Light my touch on your shoulder-blade.

Sancta Hilda, Myfanwyatia
   Evansensis – I hold your heart,
Willowy banks of a willowy Cherwell a
   Willowy figure with lips apart,
Strong and willowy, strong to pillow me,
   Gold Myfanwy, kisses and art.

Tubular bells of tall St. Barnabas,
   Single clatter above St. Paul,
Chasuble, acolyte, incense-offering,
   Spectacled faces held in thrall.
There in the nimbus and Comper tracery
   Gold Myfanwy blesses us all.

Gleam of gas upon Oxford station,
   Gleam of gas on her straight gold hair,
Hair flung back with an ostentation,
   Waiting alone for a girl friend there.
Second in Mods and a Third in Theology
   Come to breathe again Oxford air.

*Her* Myfanwy as in Cadena days,
*Her* Myfanwy, a schoolgirl voice,
Tentative brush of a cheek in a cocoa crush,
Coffee and Ulysses, Tennyson, Joyce,
Alpha-minded and other dimensional,
Freud or Calvary? Take your choice.

*Her* Myfanwy? *My* Myfanwy.
Bicycle bells in a Boar's Hill Pine,
Stedman Triple from All Saints' steeple,
Tom and his hundred and one at nine,
Bells of Butterfield, caught in Keble,
Sally and backstroke answer "*Mine!*"

## In a Bath Teashop

"Let us not speak, for the love we bear one another –
    Let us hold hands and look."
She, such a very ordinary little woman;
    He, such a thumping crook;
But both, for a moment, little lower than the angels
    In the teashop's ingle-nook.

## Senex

Oh would I could subdue the flesh
   Which sadly troubles me!
And then perhaps could view the flesh
As though I never knew the flesh
   And merry misery.

To see the golden hiking girl
   With wind about her hair,
The tennis-playing, biking girl,
The wholly-to-my-liking girl,
   To see and not to care.

At sundown on my tricycle
  I tour the Borough's edge,
And icy as an icicle
See bicycle by bicycle
  Stacked waiting in the hedge.

Get down from me! I thunder there,
  You spaniels! Shut your jaws!
Your teeth are stuffed with underwear,
Suspenders torn asunder there
  And buttocks in your paws!

Oh whip the dogs away my Lord,
  They make me ill with lust.
Bend bare knees down to pray, my Lord,
Teach sulky lips to say, my Lord,
  That flaxen hair is dust.

## A Subaltern's Love-song

Miss J. Hunter Dunn, Miss J. Hunter Dunn,
Furnish'd and burnish'd by Aldershot sun,
What strenuous singles we played after tea,
We in the tournament – you against me!

Love-thirty, love-forty, oh! weakness of joy,
The speed of a swallow, the grace of a boy,
With carefullest carelessness, gaily you won,
I am weak from your loveliness, Joan Hunter Dunn.

Miss Joan Hunter Dunn, Miss Joan Hunter Dunn,
How mad I am, sad I am, glad that you won.
The warm-handled racket is back in its press,
But my shock-headed victor, she loves me no less.

Her father's euonymus shines as we walk,
And swing past the summer-house, buried in talk,
And cool the verandah that welcomes us in
To the six-o'clock news and a lime-juice and gin.

The scent of the conifers, sound of the bath,
The view from my bedroom of moss-dappled path,
As I struggle with double-end evening tie,
For we dance at the Golf Club, my victor and I.

On the floor of her bedroom lie blazer and shorts
And the cream-coloured walls are be-trophied with sports,
And westering, questioning settles the sun
On your low-leaded window, Miss Joan Hunter Dunn.

The Hillman is waiting, the light's in the hall,
The pictures of Egypt are bright on the wall,
My sweet, I am standing beside the oak stair
And there on the landing's the light on your hair.

By roads "not adopted", by woodlanded ways,
She drove to the club in the late summer haze,
Into nine-o'clock Camberley, heavy with bells
And mushroomy, pine-woody, evergreen smells.

Miss Joan Hunter Dunn, Miss Joan Hunter Dunn,
I can hear from the car-park the dance has begun.
Oh! full Surrey twilight! importunate band!
Oh! strongly adorable tennis-girl's hand!

Around us are Rovers and Austins afar,
Above us, the intimate roof of the car,
And here on my right is the girl of my choice,
With the tilt of her nose and the chime of her voice,

And the scent of her wrap, and the words never said,
And the ominous, ominous dancing ahead.
We sat in the car park till twenty to one
And now I'm engaged to Miss Joan Hunter Dunn.

## Invasion Exercise on the Poultry Farm

Softly croons the radiogram, loudly hoot the owls,
Judy gives the door a slam and goes to feed the fowls.
Marty rolls a Craven A around her ruby lips
And runs her yellow fingers down her corduroyded hips,
Shuts her mouth and screws her eyes and puffs her fag alight
And hears some most peculiar cries that echo through the night.
Ting-a-ling the telephone, to-whit to-whoo the owls,
Judy, Judy, Judy girl, and have you fed the fowls?
No answer as the poultry gate is swinging there ajar.
Boom the bombers overhead, between the clouds a star,
And just outside, among the arks, in a shadowy sheltered place
Lie Judy and a paratroop in horrible embrace.
Ting-a-ling the telephone. "Yes, this is Marty Hayne."
"Have you seen a paratroop come walking down your lane?
He may be on your premises, he may be somewhere near,
And if he is report the fact to Major Maxton-Weir."

*Marty moves in dread towards the window – standing there*
*Draws the curtain – sees the guilty movement of the pair.*[1]
White with rage and lined with age but strong and sturdy still
Marty now co-ordinates her passions and her will,
*She* will teach that Judy girl to trifle with the heart
And go and kiss a paratroop like any common tart.
She switches up the radiogram and covered by the blare
She goes and gets a riding whip and whirls it in the air,
She fetches down a length of rope and rushes, breathing hard
To let the couple have it for embracing in the yard.
Crack! the pair are paralysed. Click! they cannot stir.
Zip! she's trussed the paratroop. There's no embracing *her*.
"Hullo, hullo, hullo, hullo . . . Major Maxton-Weir?
I've trussed your missing paratroop. He's waiting for you here."

[1] These lines in italic are by Henry Oscar.

## The Irish Unionist's Farewell to Greta Hellstrom in 1922

Golden haired and golden hearted
   I would ever have you be,
As you were when last we parted
   Smiling slow and sad at me.
Oh! the fighting down of passion!
   Oh! the century-seeming pain –
Parting in this off-hand fashion
   In Dungarvan in the rain.

Slanting eyes of blue, unweeping,
   Stands my Swedish beauty where
Gusts of Irish rain are sweeping
   Round the statue in the square;
Corner boys against the walling
   Watch us furtively in vain,
And the Angelus is calling
   Through Dungarvan in the rain.

Gales along the Commeragh Mountains,
   Beating sleet on creaking signs,
Iron gutters turned to fountains,
   And the windscreen laced with lines,
And the evening getting later,
   And the ache – increased again,
As the distance grows the greater
   From Dungarvan in the rain.

There is no one now to wonder
What eccentric sits in state
While the beech trees rock and thunder
Round his gate-lodge and his gate.
Gone – the ornamental plaster,
Gone – the overgrown demesne
And the car goes fast, and faster,
From Dungarvan in the rain.

Had I kissed and drawn you to me,
Had you yielded warm for cold,
What a power had pounded through me
As I stroked your streaming gold!
You were right to keep us parted:
Bound and parted we remain,
Aching, if unbroken hearted –
Oh! Dungarvan in the rain.

## Indoor Games near Newbury

In among the silver birches winding ways of tarmac wander
   And the signs to Bussock Bottom, Tussock Wood and Windy Brake,
Gabled lodges, tile-hung churches, catch the lights of our Lagonda
   As we drive to Wendy's party, lemon curd and Christmas cake.
      Rich the makes of motor whirring,
      Past the pine-plantation purring
         Come up, Hupmobile, Delage!
      Short the way your chauffeurs travel,
      Crunching over private gravel
         Each from out his warm garáge.

Oh but Wendy, when the carpet yielded to my indoor pumps
      There you stood, your gold hair streaming,
      Handsome in the hall-light gleaming
There you looked and there you led me off into the game of clumps
      Then the new Victrola playing
      And your funny uncle saying
"Choose your partners for a fox-trot! Dance until its *tea* o'clock!
      "Come on, young 'uns, foot it featly!"
      Was it chance that paired us neatly,
      I, who loved you so completely,
You, who pressed me closely to you, hard against your party frock?"

"Meet me when you've finished eating!" So we met and no one found us.
Oh that dark and furry cupboard while the rest played hide and seek!
Holding hands our two hearts beating in the bedroom silence round us,
Holding hands and hardly hearing sudden footstep, thud and shriek.
Love that lay too deep for kissing –
"Where *is* Wendy? Wendy's missing!"
Love so pure it *had* to end,
Love so strong that I was frighten'd
When you gripped my fingers tight and
Hugging, whispered "I'm your friend."

Goodbye Wendy! Send the fairies, pinewood elf and larch tree gnome,
    Spingle-spangled stars are peeping
    At the lush Lagonda creeping
Down the winding ways of tarmac to the leaded lights of home.
    There, among the silver birches,
    All the bells of all the churches
Sounded in the bath-waste running out into the frosty air.
    Wendy speeded my undressing,
    Wendy is the sheet's caressing
    Wendy bending gives a blessing,
Holds me as I drift to dreamland, safe inside my slumber-wear.

## Narcissus

Yes, it was Bedford Park the vision came from –
  de Morgan lustre glowing round the hearth,
And that sweet flower which self-love takes its name from
  Nodding among the lilies in the garth,
And Arnold Dolmetsch touching the spinet,
And Mother, Chiswick's earliest suffragette.

I was a delicate boy – my parents' only –
  And highly strung. My father was in trade.
And how I loved, when Mother left me lonely,
  To watch old Martha spice the marmalade,
Or help with flower arrangements in the lobby
Before I went to find my playmate Bobby.

We'ld go for walks, we bosom boyfriends would
  (For Bobby's watching sisters drove us mad),
And when we just did nothing we were good,
  But when we touched each other we were bad.
I found this out when Mother said one day
She thought we were unwholesome in our play.

So Bobby and I were parted. Bobby dear,
  I didn't want my tea. I heard your sisters
Playing at hide-and-seek with you quite near
  As off the garden gate I picked the blisters.
Oh tell me, Mother, what I mustn't do –
Then, Bobby, I can play again with you.

For I know hide-and-seek's most secret places
  More than your sisters do. And you and I
Can scramble into them and leave no traces,
  Nothing above us but the twigs and sky,
Nothing below us but the leaf-mould chilly
Where we can warm and hug each other silly.

My Mother wouldn't tell me why she hated
  The things we did, and why they pained her so.
She said a fate far worse than death awaited
  People who did the things we didn't know,
And then she said I was her precious child,
And once there was a man called Oscar Wilde.

"Open your story book and find a tale
   Of ladyes fayre and deeds of derring-do,
Or good Sir Gawaine and the Holy Grail,
   Mother will read her boy a page or two
Before she goes, this Women's Suffrage Week,
To hear that clever Mrs. Pankhurst speak.

Sleep with your hands above your head. That's right –
   And let no evil thoughts pollute the dark."
She rose, and lowered the incandescent light.
   I heard her footsteps die down Bedford Park.
Mother where are you? Bobby, Bobby, where?
I clung for safety to my teddy bear.

## *From* North Coast Recollections

Four macrocarpa hide the tennis club.
Two children of a chartered actuary
(Beaworthy, Trouncer, Heppelwhite and Co.),
Harold and Bonzo Trouncer are engaged
In semi-finals for the tournament.
"Love thirty!" Pang! across the evening air
Twangs Harold's racquet. Plung! the ball returns.
Experience at Budleigh Salterton
Keeps Bonzo steady at the net. "Well done!"
"Love forty!" Captain Mycroft, midst applause,
Pronounces for the Trouncers, to be sure
He can't be certain Bonzo didn't reach
A shade across the net, but Demon Sex,
That tulip figure in white cotton dress,
Bare legs, wide eyes and so tip-tilted nose
Quite overset him. Harold serves again
And Mrs. Pardon says it's getting cold,
Miss Myatt shivers, Lady Lambourn thinks
These English evenings are a little damp
And dreams herself again in fair Shanghai.
"Game . . . AND ! and thank you!"; so the pair from Rock
(A neighbouring and less exclusive place)
Defeated, climb into their Morris Ten.
"The final is to-morrow! Well, good night!"

He lay in wait, he lay in wait, he did,
John Lambourn, curly-headed; dewy grass
Dampened his flannels, but he still remained.

The sunset drained the colours black and gold,
From his all-glorious First Eleven scarf.
But still he waited by the twilit hedge.
Only his eyes blazed blue with early love,
Blue blazing in the darkness of the lane,
Blue blazer, less incalculably blue,
Dark scarf, white flannels, supple body still,
First love, first light, first life. A heartbeat noise!
His heart or little feet? A snap of twigs
Dry, dead and brown the under branches part
And Bonzo scrambles by their secret way.
First love so deep, John Lambourn cannot speak,
So deep, he feels a tightening in his throat,
So tender, he could brush away the sand
Dried up in patches on her freckled legs,
Could hold her gently till the stars went down,
And if she cut herself would staunch the wound,
Yes, even with this First Eleven scarf,
And hold it there for hours.

So happy, and so deep he loves the world,
Could worship God and rocks and stones and trees,
Be nicer to his mother, kill himself
If that would make him pure enough for her.
And so at last he manages to say
"You going to the Hanks's hop to-night?"
"Well, I'm not sure. Are you?" "I think I may –
"It's pretty dud though, – only lemonade."

*Sir Gawaint was a right and goodly knight*
*Nor ever wist he to uncurtis be.*
So old, so lovely, and so very true!
Then Mrs. Wilder shut the Walter Crane
And tied the tapes and tucked her youngest in
What time without amidst the lavender
At late last 'He' played Primula and Prue
With new-found liveliness, for bed was soon.

And in the garage, serious seventeen
Harvey, the eldest, hammered on, content,
Fixing a mizzen to his model boat.
"Coo-ee! Coo-ee!" across the lavender,
Across the mist of pale gypsophila
And lolling purple poppies, Mumsie called,
A splendid sunset lit the rocking-horse
And Morris pattern of the nursery walls.
"Coo-ee!" the slate-hung, goodly-builded house
And sunset-sodden garden fell to quiet.
"Prue! Primsie! Mumsie wants you. Sleepi-byes!"
Prue jumped the marigolds and hid herself,
Her sister scampered to the Wendy Hut
And Harvey, glancing at his Ingersoll,
Thought "Damn! I must get ready for the dance."

## The Olympic Girl

The sort of girl I like to see
Smiles down from her great height at me.
She stands in strong, athletic pose
And wrinkles her *retroussé* nose.
Is it distaste that makes her frown,
So furious and freckled, down
On an unhealthy worm like me?
Or am I what she likes to see?
I do not know, though much I care.
*εἴθε γενοίμην* . . . would I were
(Forgive me, shade of Rupert Brooke)
An object fit to claim her look.
Oh! would I were her racket press'd
With hard excitement to her breast
And swished into the sunlit air
Arm-high above her tousled hair,
And banged against the bounding ball
"Oh! Plung!" my tauten'd strings would call,
"Oh! Plung! my darling, break my strings
For you I will do brilliant things."

And when the match is over, I
Would flop beside you, hear you sigh;
And then, with what supreme caress,
You'ld tuck me up into my press.
Fair tigress of the tennis courts,
So short in sleeve and strong in shorts,
Little, alas, to you I mean,
For I am bald and old and green.

## The Licorice Fields at Pontefract

In the licorice fields at Pontefract
   My love and I did meet
And many a burdened licorice bush
   Was blooming round our feet;
Red hair she had and golden skin,
Her sulky lips were shaped for sin,
Her sturdy legs were flannel-slack'd,
The strongest legs in Pontefract.

The light and dangling licorice flowers
   Gave off the sweetest smells;
From various black Victorian towers
   The Sunday evening bells
Came pealing over dales and hills
And tanneries and silent mills
And lowly streets where country stops
And little shuttered corner shops.

She cast her blazing eyes on me
  And plucked a licorice leaf;
I was her captive slave and she
  My red-haired robber chief.
Oh love! for love I could not speak,
It left me winded, wilting, weak
And held in brown arms strong and bare
And wound with flaming ropes of hair.

## Slough

Come, friendly bombs, and fall on Slough
It isn't fit for humans now,
There isn't grass to graze a cow
    Swarm over, Death!

Come, bombs, and blow to smithereens
Those air-conditioned, bright canteens,
Tinned fruit, tinned meat, tinned milk, tinned beans
    Tinned minds, tinned breath.

Mess up the mess they call a town –
A house for ninety-seven down
And once a week a half-a-crown
    For twenty years,

And get that man with double chin
Who'll always cheat and always win,
Who washes his repulsive skin
    In women's tears,

And smash his desk of polished oak
And smash his hands so used to stroke
And stop his boring dirty joke
    And make him yell.

But spare the bald young clerks who add
The profits of the stinking cad;
It's not their fault that they are mad,
They've tasted Hell.

It's not their fault they do not know
The birdsong from the radio,
It's not their fault they often go
To Maidenhead

And talk of sports and makes of cars
In various bogus Tudor bars
And daren't look up and see the stars
But belch instead.

In labour-saving homes, with care
Their wives frizz out peroxide hair
And dry it in synthetic air
And paint their nails.

Come, friendly bombs, and fall on Slough
To get it ready for the plough.
The cabbages are coming now;
The earth exhales.

## A Russell Flint

I could not speak for amazement at your beauty
As you came down the Garrick stair,
Grey-green eyes like the turbulent Atlantic
And floppy schoolgirl hair.

I could see you in a Sussex teashop,
Dressed in peasant weave and brogues,
Turning over, as firelight shone on brassware,
Last year's tea-stained *Vogues*.

I could see you as a large-eyed student,
  Frowning as you tried to learn,
Or, head flung back, the confident girl prefect,
  Thrillingly kind and stern.

I could not speak for amazement at your beauty;
  Yet, when you spoke to me,
You were calm and gentle as a rock pool
  Waiting, warm, for the sea.

Wave on wave, I plunged in them to meet you –
  In wave on wave I drown;
Calm rock pool, on the shore of my security
  Hold me when the tide goes down.

## Agricultural Caress

Keep me from Thelma's sister Pearl!
She puts my senses in a whirl,
Weakens my knees and keeps me waiting
Until my heart stops palpitating.

The debs may turn disdainful backs
On Pearl's uncouth mechanic slacks,
And outraged see the fire that lies
And smoulders in her long-lashed eyes.

Have they such weather-freckled features,
The smooth sophisticated creatures?
Ah, not to them such limbs belong,
Such animal movements sure and strong,

Such arms to take a man and press
In agricultural caress
His head to hers, and hold him there
Deep buried in her chestnut hair.

God shrive me from this morning lust
For supple farm girls: if you must,
Send the cold daughter of an earl –
But spare me Thelma's sister Pearl!

## The Cockney Amorist

Oh when my love, my darling,
  You've left me here alone,
I'll walk the streets of London
  Which once seemed all our own.

The vast suburban churches
  Together we have found:
The ones which smelt of gaslight
  The ones in incense drown'd;
I'll use them now for praying in
  And not for looking round.

No more the Hackney Empire
  Shall find us in its stalls
When on the limelit crooner
  The thankful curtain falls,
And soft electric lamplight
  Reveals the gilded walls.

I will not go to Finsbury Park
 The putting course to see
Nor cross the crowded High Road
 To Williamsons' to tea,
For these and all the other things
 Were part of you and me.

I love you, oh my darling,
 And what I can't make out
Is why since you have left me
 I'm somehow still about.

## Hearts Together

How emerald the chalky depths
   Below the Dancing Ledge!
We pulled the jelly-fishes up
   And threw them in the hedge
That with its stones and sea-pink tufts
   Ran to the high cliff edge.

And lucky was the jelly-fish
   That melted in the sun
And poured its vitals on the turf
   In self-effacing fun,
Like us who in each other's arms
   Were seed and soul in one.

O rational the happy bathe
   An hour before our tea,
When you were swimming breast-stroke, all
   Along the rocking sea
And, in between the waves, explain'd
   The Universe to me.

The Dorset sun stream'd on our limbs
   And scorch'd our hinder parts:
We gazed into the pebble beach
   And so discussed the arts,
O logical and happy we
   Emancipated hearts.

## Lenten Thoughts of a High Anglican

Isn't she lovely, 'the Mistress'?
With her wide-apart grey-green eyes,
The droop of her lips and, when she smiles,
Her glance of amused surprise?

How nonchalantly she wears her clothes,
How expensive they are as well!
And the sound of her voice is as soft and deep
As the Christ Church tenor bell.

But why do I call her 'the Mistress'
Who know not her way of life?
Because she has more of a cared-for air
Than many a legal wife.

How elegantly she swings along
In the vapoury incense veil;
The angel choir must pause in song
When she kneels at the altar rail.

The parson said that we shouldn't stare
Around when we come to church,
Or the Unknown God we are seeking
May forever elude our search.

But I hope the preacher will not think
   It unorthodox and odd
If I add that I glimpse in 'the Mistress'
   A hint of the Unknown God.

[This is about a lady I see on Sunday
mornings in a London church.]

# CHURCH

## Hymn

The Church's Restoration
In eighteen-eighty-three
Has left for contemplation
Not what there used to be.
How well the ancient woodwork
Looks round the Rect'ry hall,
Memorial of the good work
Of him who plann'd it all.

He who took down the pew-ends
And sold them anywhere
But kindly spared a few ends
Work'd up into a chair.
O worthy persecution
Of dust! O hue divine!
O cheerful substitution,
Thou varnishéd pitch-pine!

Church furnishing! Church furnishing!
Sing art and crafty praise!
He gave the brass for burnishing
He gave the thick red baize,
He gave the new addition,
Pull'd down the dull old aisle,
– To pave the sweet transition
He gave th' encaustic tile.

Of marble brown and veinéd
He did the pulpit make;
He order'd windows stainéd
Light red and crimson lake.
Sing on, with hymns uproarious,
Ye humble and aloof,
Look up! and oh how glorious
He has restored the roof!

## In Westminster Abbey

Let me take this other glove off
   As the *vox humana* swells,
And the beauteous fields of Eden
   Bask beneath the Abbey bells.
Here, where England's statesmen lie,
Listen to a lady's cry.

Gracious Lord, oh bomb the Germans.
   Spare their women for Thy Sake,
And if that is not too easy
   We will pardon Thy Mistake.
But, gracious Lord, whate'er shall be,
Don't let anyone bomb me.

Keep our Empire undismembered
   Guide our Forces by Thy Hand,
Gallant blacks from far Jamaica,
   Honduras and Togoland;
Protect them Lord in all their fights,
And, even more, protect the whites.

Think of what our Nation stands for,
   Books from Boots' and country lanes,
Free speech, free passes, class distinction,
   Democracy and proper drains.
Lord, put beneath Thy special care
One-eighty-nine Cadogan Square.

VISCOUNT PALMERSTON

Although dear Lord I am a sinner,
  I have done no major crime;
Now I'll come to Evening Service
  Whensoever I have the time.
So, Lord, reserve for me a crown,
And do not let my shares go down.

I will labour for Thy Kingdom,
  Help our lads to win the war,
Send white feathers to the cowards
  Join the Women's Army Corps,
Then wash the Steps around Thy Throne
In the Eternal Safety Zone.

Now I feel a little better,
  What a treat to hear Thy Word,
Where the bones of leading statesmen,
  Have so often been interr'd.
And now, dear Lord, I cannot wait
Because I have a luncheon date.

## Church of England thoughts occasioned by hearing the bells of Magdalen Tower from the Botanic Garden, Oxford on St. Mary Magdalen's Day

I see the urn against the yew,
  The sunlit urn of sculptured stone,
I see its shapely shadow fall
On this enormous garden wall
  Which makes a kingdom of its own.

A grassy kingdom sweet to view
  With tiger lilies still in flower
And beds of umbelliferae
Ranged in Linnaean symmetry,
  All in the sound of Magdalen Tower.

A multiplicity of bells,
  A changing cadence, rich and deep
Swung from those pinnacles on high
To fill the trees and flood the sky
  And rock the sailing clouds to sleep.

A Church of England sound, it tells
  Of "moderate" worship, God and State,
Where matins congregations go
Conservative and good and slow
  To elevations of the plate.

And loud through resin-scented chines
  And purple rhododendrons roll'd,
I hear the bells for Eucharist
From churches blue with incense mist
  Where reredoses twinkle gold.

Chapels-of-ease by railway lines
  And humble streets and smells of gas
I hear your plaintive ting-tangs call
From many a gabled western wall
  To Morning Prayer or Holy Mass.

In country churches old and pale
  I hear the changes smoothly rung
And watch the coloured sallies fly
From rugged hands to rafters high
  As round and back the bells are swung.

Before the spell begin to fail,
  Before the bells have lost their power,
Before the grassy kingdom fade
And Oxford traffic roar invade,
  I thank the bells of Magdalen Tower.

## Bristol

Green upon the flooded Avon shone the after-storm-wet-sky
Quick the struggling withy branches let the leaves of autumn fly
And a star shone over Bristol, wonderfully far and high.

Ringers in an oil-lit belfry – Bitton? Kelston? who shall say? –
Smoothly practising a plain course, caverned out the dying day
As their melancholy music flooded up and ebbed away.

Then all Somerset was round me and I saw the clippers ride,
High above the moonlit houses, triple-masted on the tide,
By the tall embattled church-towers of the Bristol waterside.

And an undersong to branches dripping into pools and wells
Out of multitudes of elm trees over leagues of hills and dells
Was the mathematic pattern of a plain course on the bells.*

| * | | | | | | | | | | |
|---|---|---|---|---|---|---|---|---|---|---|
| 1 | 2 | 2 | 4 | 4 | 5 | 5 | 3 | 3 | 1 | 1 |
| 2 | 1 | 4 | 2 | 5 | 4 | 3 | 5 | 1 | 3 | 2 |
| 3 | 4 | 1 | 5 | 2 | 3 | 4 | 1 | 5 | 2 | 3 |
| 4 | 3 | 5 | 1 | 3 | 2 | 1 | 4 | 2 | 5 | 4 |
| 5 | 5 | 3 | 3 | 1 | 1 | 2 | 2 | 4 | 4 | 5 |

## A Lincolnshire Tale

Kirkby with Muckby-cum-Sparrowby-cum-Spinx
Is down a long lane in the county of Lincs,
And often on Wednesdays, well-harnessed and spruce,
I would drive into Wiss over Winderby Sluice.

A whacking great sunset bathed level and drain
From Kirkby with Muckby to Beckby-on-Bain,
And I saw, as I journeyed, my marketing done
Old Caistorby tower take the last of the sun.

The night air grew nippy. An autumn mist roll'd
(In a scent of dead cabbages) down from the wold,
In the ocean of silence that flooded me round
The crunch of the wheels was a comforting sound.

The lane lengthened narrowly into the night
With the Bain on its left bank, the drain on its right,
And feebly the carriage-lamps glimmered ahead
When all of a sudden *the pony fell dead.*

The remoteness was awful, the stillness intense,
Of invisible fenland, around and immense;
And out of the dark, with a roar and a swell,
Swung, hollowly thundering, Speckleby bell.

Though myself the Archdeacon for many a year,
I had not summoned courage for visiting here;
Our incumbents were mostly eccentric or sad
But – *the Speckleby Rector was said to be mad.*

Oh cold was the ev'ning and tall was the tower
And strangely compelling the tenor bell's power!
As loud on the reed-beds and strong through the dark
It toll'd from the church in the tenantless park.

The mansion was ruined, the empty demesne
Was slowly reverting to marshland again –
Marsh where the village was, grass in the Hall,
And the church and the Rectory waiting to fall.

And even in springtime with kingcups about
And stumps of old oak-trees attempting to sprout,
'Twas a sinister place, neither fenland nor wold,
And doubly forbidding in darkness and cold.

As down swung the tenor, a beacon of sound,
Over listening acres of waterlogged ground
I stood by the tombs to see pass and repass
The gleam of a taper, through clear leaded glass,

And such lighting of lights in the thunderous roar
That heart summoned courage to hand at the door;
I grated it open on scents I knew well,
The dry smell of damp rot, the hassocky smell.

What a forest of woodwork in ochres and grains
Unevenly doubled in diamonded panes,
And over the plaster, so textured with time,
Sweet discoloration of umber and lime.

The candles ensconced on each high pannelled pew
Brought the caverns of brass-studded baize into view,
But the roof and its rafters were lost to the sight
As they soared to the dark of the Lincolnshire night:

And high from the chancel arch paused to look down
A sign-painter's beasts in their fight for the Crown,
While massive, impressive, and still as the grave
A three-decker pulpit frowned over the nave.

Shall I ever forget what a stillness was there
When the bell ceased its tolling and thinned on the air?
Then an opening door showed a long pair of hands
And the Rector himself in his gown and his bands.

*     *     *     *     *

Such a fell Visitation I shall not forget,
Such a rush through the dark, that I rush through it yet,
And I pray, as the bells ring o'er fenland and hill,
That the Speckleby acres be tenantless still.

## St. Saviour's, Aberdeen Park, Highbury, London, N.

With oh such peculiar branching and over-reaching of wire
   Trolley-bus standards pick their threads from the London sky
Diminishing up the perspective, Highbury-bound retire
   Threads and buses and standards with plane trees volleying by
And, more peculiar still, that ever-increasing spire
   Bulges over the housetops, polychromatic and high.

Stop the trolley-bus, stop! And here, where the roads unite
   Of weariest worn-out London – no cigarettes, no beer,
No repairs undertaken, nothing in stock – alight;
   For over the waste of willow-herb, look at her, sailing clear,
A great Victorian church, tall, unbroken and bright
   In a sun that's setting in Willesden and saturating us here.

These were the streets my parents knew when they loved and won –
   The brougham that crunched the gravel, the laurel-girt paths that wind,
Geranium-beds for the lawn, Venetian blinds for the sun,
   A separate tradesman's entrance, straw in the mews behind,
Just in the four-mile radius where hackney carriages run,
   Solid Italianate houses for the solid commercial mind.

These were the streets they knew; and I, by descent, belong
   To these tall neglected houses divided into flats.
Only the church remains, where carriages used to throng
   And my mother stepped out in flounces and my father stepped out in spats
To shadowy stained-glass matins or gas-lit evensong
   And back in a country quiet with doffing of chimney hats.

Great red church of my parents, cruciform crossing they knew –
Over these same encaustics they and their parents trod
Bound through a red-brick transept for a once familiar pew
Where the organ set them singing and the sermon let them nod
And up this coloured brickwork the same long shadows grew
As these in the stencilled chancel where I kneel in the presence of God.

Wonder beyond Time's wonders, that Bread so white and small
Veiled in golden curtains, too mighty for men to see,
Is the Power which sends the shadows up this polychrome wall,
Is God who created the present, the chain-smoking millions and me;
Beyond the throb of the engines is the throbbing heart of all –
Christ, at this Highbury altar, I offer myself To Thee.

## A Lincolnshire Church

Greyly tremendous the thunder
Hung over the width of the wold
But here the green marsh was alight
In a huge cloud cavern of gold,
And there, on a gentle eminence,
Topping some ash trees, a tower
Silver and brown in the sunlight,
Worn by sea-wind and shower,
Lincolnshire Middle Pointed.
And around it, turning their backs,
The usual sprinkle of villas;
The usual woman in slacks,
Cigarette in her mouth,
Regretting Americans, stands
As a wireless croons in the kitchen
Manicuring her hands.

Dear old, bloody old England
Of telegraph poles and tin,
Seemingly so indifferent
And with so little soul to win.
What sort of church, I wonder?
The path is a grassy mat,
And grass is drowning the headstones
Sloping this way and that.
"Cathedral Glass" in the windows,
A roof of unsuitable slate –
Restored with a vengeance, for certain,
About eighteen-eighty-eight.
The door swung easily open
(Unlocked, for these parts, is odd)
And there on the South aisle altar
Is the tabernacle of God.
There where the white light flickers
By the white and silver veil,
A wafer dipped in a wine-drop
Is the Presence the angels hail,

Is God who created the Heavens
And the wide green marsh as well
Who sings in the sky with the skylark
Who calls in the evening bell,
Is God who prepared His coming
With fruit of the earth for his food
With stone for building His churches
And trees for making His rood.

There where the white light flickers,
Our Creator is with us yet,
To be worshipped by you and the woman
Of the slacks and the cigarette.

*     *     *     *     *

The great door shuts, and lessens
That roar of churchyard trees
And the Presence of God Incarnate
Has brought me to my knees.
"I acknowledge my transgressions"
The well-known phrases rolled
With thunder sailing over
From the heavily clouded wold.
"And my sin is ever before me."
There in the lighted East
He stood in that lowering sunlight,
An Indian Christian priest.
And why he was here in Lincolnshire
I neither asked nor knew,
Nor whether his flock was many
Nor whether his flock was few
I thought of the heaving waters
That bore him from sun glare harsh

Of some Indian Anglican Mission
To this green enormous marsh.
There where the white light flickers,
Here, as the rains descend,
The same mysterious Godhead
Is welcoming His friend.

# PEOPLE

## The 'Varsity Students' Rag

I'm afraid the fellows in Putney rather wish they had
The social ease and manners of a 'varsity undergrad,
For tho' they're awf'lly decent and up to a lark as a rule
You want to have the 'varsity touch after a public school.

CHORUS:

*We* had a rag at Monico's. *We* had a rag at the Troc.,
And the one we had at the Berkeley gave the customers quite a shock.
*Then* we went to the Popular, and after that – oh my!
I *wish* you'd seen the rag we had in the Grill Room at the Cri.

I started a rag in Putney at our Frothblower's Branch down there;
We got in a damn'd old lorry and drove to Trafalgar Square;
And we each had a couple of toy balloons and made the hell of a din,
And I saw a bobby at Parson's Green who looked like running us in.

CHORUS: We, etc.

But that's nothing to the rag we had at the college the other night;
We'd gallons and gallons of cider – and I got frightfully tight.
And then we smash'd up ev'rything, and what was the funniest part
We smashed some rotten old pictures which were priceless works of art.

CHORUS: We, etc.

There's something about a 'varsity man that distinguishes him from a cad:
You can tell by his tie and blazer he's a 'varsity undergrad,
And you know that he's always ready and up to a bit of a lark,
With a toy balloon and a whistle and some cider after dark.

CHORUS: We, etc.

## The Arrest of Oscar Wilde at the Cadogan Hotel

He sipped at a weak hock and seltzer
  As he gazed at the London skies
Through the Nottingham lace of the curtains
  Or was it his bees-winged eyes?

To the right and before him Pont Street
  Did tower in her new built red,
As hard as the morning gaslight
  That shone on his unmade bed,

"I want some more hock in my seltzer,
  And Robbie, please give me your hand –
Is this the end or beginning?
  How can I understand?

"So you've brought me the latest *Yellow Book*:
  And Buchan has got in it now:
Approval of what is approved of
  Is as false as a well-kept vow.

"More hock, Robbie – where is the seltzer?
  Dear boy, pull again at the bell!
They are all little better than *cretins*,
  Though this *is* the Cadogan Hotel.

"One astrakhan coat is at Willis's –
  Another one's at the Savoy:
Do fetch my morocco portmanteau,
  And bring them on later, dear boy."

A thump, and a murmur of voices –
  ("Oh why must they make such a din?")
As the door of the bedroom swung open
  And TWO PLAIN CLOTHES POLICEMEN came in:

"Mr. Woilde, we 'ave come for tew take yew
  Where felons and criminals dwell:
We must ask yew tew leave with us quoietly
  For this *is* the Cadogan Hotel."

He rose, and he put down *The Yellow Book*.
  He staggered – and, terrible-eyed,
He brushed past the palms on the staircase
  And was helped to a hansom outside.

## The Planster's Vision

Cut down that timber! Bells, too many and strong,
Pouring their music through the branches bare,
From moon-white church-towers down the windy air
Have pealed the centuries out with Evensong.
Remove those cottages, a huddled throng!
Too many babies have been born in there,
Too many coffins, bumping down the stair,
Carried the old their garden paths along.

I have a Vision of The Future, chum,
The workers' flats in fields of soya beans
Tower up like silver pencils, score on score:
And Surging Millions hear the Challenge come
From microphones in communal canteens
"No Right! No Wrong! All's perfect, evermore."

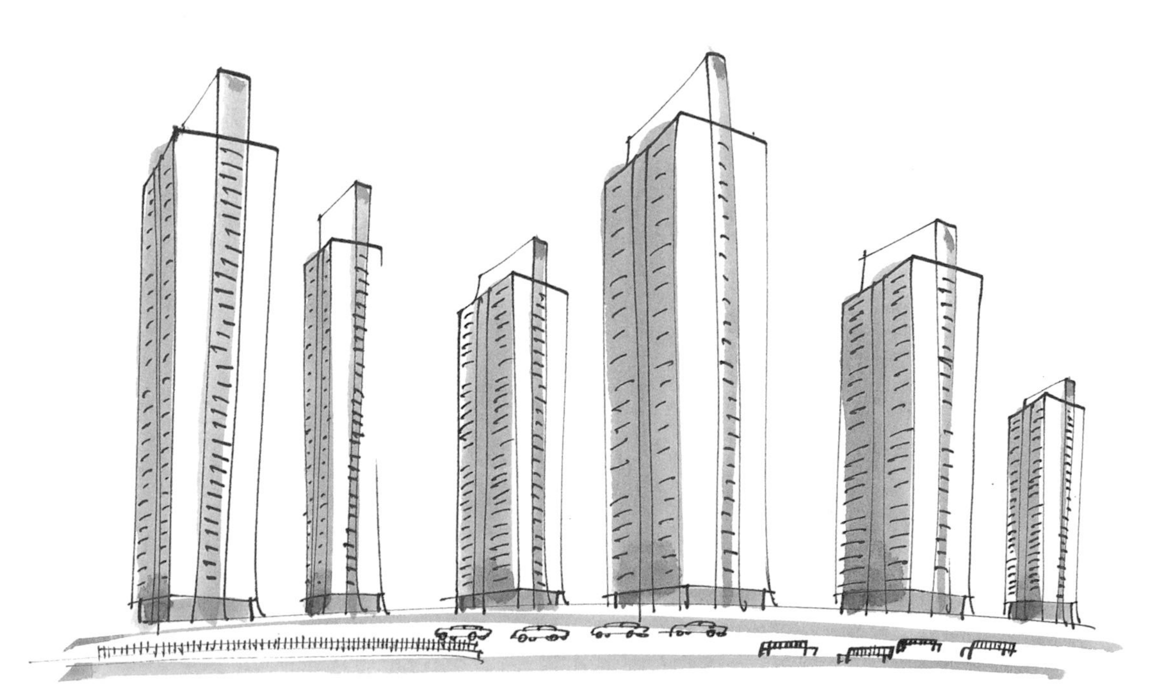

# Youth and Age on Beaulieu River, Hants

Early sun on Beaulieu water
Lights the undersides of oaks,
Clumps of leaves it floods and blanches,
All transparent glow the branches
Which the double sunlight soaks;
To her craft on Beaulieu water
Clemency the General's daughter
Pulls across with even strokes.

Schoolboy-sure she is this morning;
Soon her sharpie's rigg'd and free.
Cool beneath a garden awning
Mrs. Fairclough, sipping tea
And raising large long-distance glasses
As the little sharpie passes,
Sighs our sailor girl to see:

Tulip figure, so appealing,
Oval face, so serious-eyed,
Tree-roots pass'd and muddy beaches.
On to huge and lake-like reaches,
Soft and sun-warm, see her glide –
Slacks the slim young limbs revealing,
Sun-brown arm the tiller feeling –
With the wind and with the tide.

Evening light will bring the water,
Day-long sun will burst the bud,
Clemency, the General's daughter,
Will return upon the flood.
But the older woman only
Knows the ebb-tide leaves her lonely
With the shining fields of mud.

## Sun and Fun

SONG OF A NIGHT-CLUB PROPRIETRESS

I walked into the night-club in the morning;
   There was kummel on the handle of the door.
The ashtrays were unemptied,
The cleaning unattempted,
   And a squashed tomato sandwich on the floor.

I pulled aside the thick magenta curtains
   – So Regency, so Regency, my dear –
And a host of little spiders
Ran a race across the ciders
   To a box of baby 'pollies by the beer.

Oh sun upon the summer-going by-pass
   Where ev'rything is speeding to the sea,
And wonder beyond wonder
That here where lorries thunder
   The sun should ever percolate to me.

When Boris used to call in his Sedanca,
   When Teddy took me down to his estate
When my nose excited passion,
When my clothes were in the fashion,
   When my beaux were never cross if I was late,

There was sun enough for lazing upon beaches,
   There was fun enough for far into the night.
But I'm dying now and done for,
What on earth was all the fun for?
   For I'm old and ill and terrified and tight.

## Business Girls

From the geyser ventilators
    Autumn winds are blowing down
On a thousand business women
    Having baths in Camden Town.

Waste pipes chuckle into runnels,
    Steam's escaping here and there,
Morning trains through Camden cutting
    Shake the Crescent and the Square.

Early nip of changeful autumn,
   Dahlias glimpsed through garden doors,
At the back precarious bathrooms
   Jutting out from upper floors;

And behind their frail partitions
   Business women lie and soak,
Seeing through the draughty skylight
   Flying clouds and railway smoke.

Rest you there, poor unbelov'd ones,
   Lap your loneliness in heat.
All too soon the tiny breakfast,
   Trolley-bus and windy street!

## Hunter Trials

It's awf'lly bad luck on Diana,
   Her ponies have swallowed their bits;
She fished down their throats with a spanner
   And frightened them all into fits.

So now she's attempting to borrow.
   *Do* lend her some bits, Mummy, *do*;
I'll lend her my own for to-morrow,
   But to-day *I*'ll be wanting them too.

Just look at Prunella on Guzzle,
   The wizardest pony on earth;
Why doesn't she slacken his muzzle
   And tighten the breech in his girth?

I say, Mummy, there's Mrs. Geyser
   And doesn't she look pretty sick?
I bet it's because Mona Lisa
   Was hit on the hock with a brick.

Miss Blewitt says Monica threw it,
   But Monica says it was Joan,
And Joan's very thick with Miss Blewitt,
   So Monica's sulking alone.

And Margaret failed in her paces,
  Her withers got tied in a noose,
So her coronets caught in the traces
  And now all her fetlocks are loose.

Oh, it's me now. I'm terribly nervous.
  I wonder if Smudges will shy.
She's practically certain to swerve as
  Her Pelham is over one eye.

* * * * *

Oh wasn't it naughty of Smudges?
  Oh, Mummy, I'm sick with disgust.
She threw me in front of the Judges,
  And my silly old collarbone's bust.

## How to Get On in Society

Originally set as a competition in "Time and Tide"

Phone for the fish-knives, Norman
   As Cook is a little unnerved;
You kiddies have crumpled the serviettes
   And I must have things daintily served.

Are the requisites all in the toilet?
   The frills round the cutlets can wait
Till the girl has replenished the cruets
   And switched on the logs in the grate.

It's ever so close in the lounge, dear,
But the vestibule's comfy for tea
And Howard is out riding on horseback
So do come and take some with me.

Now here is a fork for your pastries
And do use the couch for your feet;
I know what I wanted to ask you –
Is trifle sufficient for sweet?

Milk and then just as it comes dear?
I'm afraid the preserve's full of stones;
Beg pardon, I'm soiling the doileys
With afternoon tea-cakes and scones.

## False Security

I remember the dread with which I at a quarter past four
Let go with a bang behind me our house front door
And, clutching a present for my dear little hostess tight,
Sailed out for the children's party into the night
Or rather the gathering night. For still some boys
In the near municipal acres were making a noise
Shuffling in fallen leaves and shouting and whistling
And running past hedges of hawthorn, spikey and bristling.
And black in the oncoming darkness stood out the trees
And pink shone the ponds in the sunset ready to freeze
And all was still and ominous waiting for dark
And the keeper was ringing his closing bell in the park
And the arc lights started to fizzle and burst into mauve
As I climbed West Hill to the great big house in The Grove,
Where the children's party was and the dear little hostess.
But halfway up stood the empty house where the ghost is
I crossed to the other side and under the arc

Made a rush for the next kind lamp-post out of the dark
And so to the next and the next till I reached the top
Where the Grove branched off to the left. Then ready to drop
I ran to the ironwork gateway of number seven
Secure at last on the lamplit fringe of Heaven.
Oh who can say how subtle and safe one feels
Shod in one's children's sandals from Daniel Neal's,
Clad in one's party clothes made of stuff from Heal's?
And who can still one's thrill at the candle shine
On cakes and ices and jelly and blackcurrant wine,
And the warm little feel of my hostess's hand in mine?
Can I forget my delight at the conjuring show?
And wasn't I proud that I was the last to go?
Too overexcited and pleased with myself to know
That the words I heard my hostess's mother employ
To a guest departing, would ever diminish my joy,
I WONDER WHERE JULIA FOUND THAT STRANGE,
RATHER COMMON LITTLE BOY?

# PLACES

## Upper Lambourne

Up the ash-tree climbs the ivy,
   Up the ivy climbs the sun,
With a twenty-thousand pattering
   Has a valley breeze begun,
Feathery ash, neglected elder,
   Shift the shade and make it run –

Shift the shade toward the nettles,
   And the nettles set it free
To streak the stained Carrara headstone
   Where, in nineteen-twenty-three,
He who trained a hundred winners
   Paid the Final Entrance Fee.

Leathery limbs of Upper Lambourne,
   Leathery skin from sun and wind,
Leathery breeches, spreading stables,
   Shining saddles left behind –
To the down the string of horses
   Moving out of sight and mind.

Feathery ash in leathery Lambourne
   Waves above the sarsen stone,
And Edwardian plantations
   So coniferously moan
As to make the swelling downland,
   Far-surrounding, seem their own.

## Uffington

Tonight we feel the muffled peal
   Hang on the village like a pall;
It overwhelms the towering elms –
   That death-reminding dying fall;
The very sky no longer high
   Comes down within the reach of all.
Imprisoned in a cage of sound
Even the trivial seems profound.

## Trebetherick

We used to picnic where the thrift
    Grew deep and tufted to the edge;
We saw the yellow foam-flakes drift
    In trembling sponges on the ledge
Below us, till the wind would lift
    Them up the cliff and o'er the hedge.
Sand in the sandwiches, wasps in the tea,
Sun on our bathing-dresses heavy with the wet,
Squelch of the bladder-wrack waiting for the sea,
Fleas round the tamarisk, an early cigarette.

From where the coastguard houses stood
    One used to see, below the hill,
The lichened branches of a wood
    In summer silver-cool and still;
And there the Shade of Evil could
    Stretch out at us from Shilla Mill.
Thick with sloe and blackberry, uneven in the light,
Lonely ran the hedge, the heavy meadow was remote,
The oldest part of Cornwall was the wood as black as night,
And the pheasant and the rabbit lay torn open at the throat.

But when a storm was at its height,
And feathery slate was black in rain,
And tamarisks were hung with light
And golden sand was brown again,
Spring tide and blizzard would unite
And sea came flooding up the lane.
Waves full of treasure then were roaring up the beach,
Ropes round our mackintoshes, waders warm and dry,
We waited for the wreckage to come swirling into reach,
Ralph, Vasey, Alastair, Biddy, John and I.

Then roller into roller curled
And thundered down the rocky bay,
And we were in a water-world
Of rain and blizzard, sea and spray,
And one against the other hurled
We struggled round to Greenaway.
Blesséd be St. Enodoc, blesséd be the wave,
Blesséd be the springy turf, we pray, pray to thee,
Ask for our children all the happy days you gave
To Ralph, Vasey, Alastair, Biddy, John and me.

## Parliament Hill Fields

Rumbling under blackened girders, Midland, bound for Cricklewood,
Puffed its sulphur to the sunset where that Land of Laundries stood.
Rumble under, thunder over, train and tram alternate go,
Shake the floor and smudge the ledger, Charrington, Sells, Dale and Co.,
Nuts and nuggets in the window, trucks along the lines below.

When the Bon Marché was shuttered, when the feet were hot and tired,
Outside Charrington's we waited, by the "STOP HERE IF REQUIRED",
Launched aboard the shopping basket, sat precipitately down,
Rocked past Zwanziger the baker's, and the terrace blackish brown,
And the curious Anglo-Norman parish church of Kentish Town.

Till the tram went over thirty, sighting terminus again,
Past municipal lawn tennis and the bobble-hanging plane;
Soft the light suburban evening caught our ashlar-speckled spire,
Eighteen-sixty Early English, as the mighty elms retire
Either side of Brookfield Mansions flashing fine French-window fire.

Oh the after-tram-ride quiet, when we heard a mile beyond,
Silver music from the bandstand, barking dogs by Highgate Pond;
Up the hill where stucco houses in Virginia creeper drown –
And my childish wave of pity, seeing children carrying down
Sheaves of drooping dandelions to the courts of Kentish Town.

## On an Old-Fashioned Water-Colour of Oxford

(Early Twentieth-Century Date)

Shines, billowing cold and gold from Cumnor Hurst,
  A winter sunset on wet cobbles, where
  By Canterbury Gate the fishtails flare.
Someone in Corpus reading for a first
Pulls down red blinds and flounders on, immers'd
  In Hegel, heedless of the yellow glare
  On porch and pinnacle and window square,
The brown stone crumbling where the skin has burst.

A late, last luncheon staggers out of Peck
  And hires a hansom: from half-flooded grass
    Returning athletes bark at what they see.
But we will mount the horse-tram's upper deck
  And wave salute to Buols', as we pass
    Bound for the Banbury Road in time for tea.

## May-Day Song for North Oxford

(Annie Laurie Tune)

Belbroughton Road is bonny, and pinkly bursts the spray
Of prunus and forsythia across the public way,
For a full spring-tide of blossom seethed and departed hence,
Leaving land-locked pools of jonquils by sunny garden fence.

And a constant sound of flushing runneth from windows where
The toothbrush too is airing in this new North Oxford air
From Summerfields to Lynam's, the thirsty tarmac dries,
And a Cherwell mist dissolveth on elm-discovering skies.

Oh! well-bound Wells and Bridges! Oh! earnest ethical search
For the wide high-table *λογος* of St. C.S. Lewis's Church.
This diamond-eyed Spring morning my soul soars up the slope
Of a right good rough-cast buttress on the housewall of my hope.

And open-necked and freckled, where once there grazed the cows,
Emancipated children swing on old apple boughs,
And pastel-shaded book rooms bring New Ideas to birth
As the whitening hawthorn only hears the heart beat of the earth.

## The Metropolitan Railway

BAKER STREET STATION BUFFET

Early Electric! With what radiant hope
   Men formed this many-branched electrolier,
Twisted the flex around the iron rope
   And let the dazzling vacuum globes hang clear,
And then with hearts the rich contrivance fill'd
Of copper, beaten by the Bromsgrove Guild.

Early Electric! Sit you down and see,
   'Mid this fine woodwork and a smell of dinner,
A stained-glass windmill and a pot of tea,
   And sepia views of leafy lanes in PINNER, –
Then visualize, far down the shining lines,
Your parents' homestead set in murmuring pines.

Smoothly from HARROW, passing PRESTON ROAD,
   They saw the last green fields and misty sky,
At NEASDEN watched a workmen's train unload,
   And, with the morning villas sliding by,
They felt so sure on their electric trip
That Youth and Progress were in partnership.

And all that day in murky London Wall
   The thought of RUISLIP kept him warm inside;
At FARRINGDON that lunch hour at a stall
   He bought a dozen plants of London Pride;
While she, in arc-lit Oxford Street adrift,
Soared through the sales by safe hydraulic lift.

Early Electric! Maybe even here
 They met that evening at six-fifteen
Beneath the hearts of this electrolier
 And caught the first non-stop to WILLESDEN GREEN,
Then out and on, through rural RAYNER'S LANE
To autumn-scented Middlesex again.

Cancer has killed him. Heart is killing her.
 The trees are down. An Odeon flashes fire
Where stood their villa by the murmuring fir
 When "they would for their children's good conspire."
Of their loves and hopes on hurrying feet
Thou art the worn memorial, Baker Street.

## Greenaway

I know so well this turfy mile,
These clumps of sea-pink withered brown,
The breezy cliff, the awkward stile,
The sandy path that takes me down.

To crackling layers of broken slate
Where black and flat sea-woodlice crawl
And isolated rock pools wait
Wash from the highest tides of all.

I know the roughly blasted track
That skirts a small and smelly bay
And over squelching bladderwrack
Leads to the beach at Greenaway.

Down on the shingle safe at last
   I hear the slowly dragging roar
As mighty rollers mount to cast
   Small coal and seaweed on the shore,

And spurting far as it can reach
   The shooting surf comes hissing round
To heave a line along the beach
   Of cowries waiting to be found.

Tide after tide by night and day
   The breakers battle with the land
And rounded smooth along the bay
   The faithful rocks protecting stand.

But in a dream the other night
  I saw this coastline from the sea
And felt the breakers plunging white
  Their weight of waters over me.

There were the stile, the turf, the shore,
  The safety line of shingle beach
With every stroke I struck the more
  The backwash sucked me out of reach.

Back into what a water-world
  Of waving weed and waiting claws?
Of writhing tentacles uncurled
  To drag me to what dreadful jaws?

## Lake District

"On their way back they found the girls at Easedale,
sitting beside the cottage where they sell ginger beer in August."

(*Peer and Heiress*, Walter Besant.)

I pass the cruet and I see the lake
Running with light, beyond the garden pine,
That lake whose waters make me dream her mine.
Up to the top board mounting for my sake,
For me she breathes, for me each soft intake,
For me the plunge, the lake and limbs combine.
I pledge her in non-alcoholic wine
And give the H.P. Sauce another shake.

Spirit of Grasmere, bells of Ambleside,
Sing you and ring you, water bells, for me;
You water-colour waterfalls may froth.
Long hiking holidays will yet provide
Long stony lanes and back at six to tea
And Heinz's ketchup on the tablecloth.

## Monody on the Death of Aldersgate Street Station

Snow falls in the buffet of Aldersgate station,
  Soot hangs in the tunnel in clouds of steam.
City of London! before the next desecration
  Let your steepled forest of churches be my theme.

Sunday Silence! with every street a dead street,
  Alley and courtyard empty and cobbled mews,
Till "tingle tang" the bell of St. Mildred's Bread Street
  Summoned the sermon taster to high box pews,

And neighbouring towers and spirelets joined the ringing
  With answering echoes from heavy commercial walls
Till all were drowned as the sailing clouds went singing
  On the roaring flood of a twelve-voiced peal from Paul's.

Then would the years fall off and Thames run slowly;
  Out into marshy meadow-land flowed the Fleet:
And the walled-in City of London, smelly and holy,
  Had a tinkling mass house in every cavernous street.

The bells rang down and St. Michael Paternoster
   Would take me into its darkness from College Hill,
Or Christ Church Newgate Street (with St. Leonard Foster)
   Would be late for Mattins and ringing insistent still.

Last of the east wall sculpture, a cherub gazes
   On broken arches, rosebay, bracken and dock,
Where once I heard the roll of the Prayer Book phrases
   And the sumptuous tick of the old west gallery clock.

Snow falls in the buffet of Aldersgate station,
   Toiling and doomed from Moorgate Street puffs the train,
For us of the steam and the gas-light, the lost generation,
   The new white cliffs of the City are built in vain.

## Hertfordshire

I had forgotten Hertfordshire,
The large unwelcome fields of roots
Where with my knickerbockered sire
I trudged in syndicated shoots;

And that unlucky day when I
Fired by mistake into the ground
Under a Lionel Edwards sky
And felt disapprobation round.

The slow drive home by motor-car,
A heavy Rover Landaulette,
Through Welwyn, Hatfield, Potters Bar,
Tweed and cigar smoke, gloom and wet:

"How many times must I explain
The way a boy should hold a gun?"
I recollect my father's pain
At such a milksop for a son.

And now I see these fields once more
Clothed, thank the Lord, in summer green,
Pale corn waves rippling to a shore
The shadowy cliffs of elm between,

Colour-washed cottages reed-thatched
And weather-boarded water mills,
Flint churches, brick and plaster patched,
On mildly undistinguished hills –

They still are there. But now the shire
   Suffers a devastating change,
Its gentle landscape strung with wire,
   Old places looking ill and strange.

One can't be sure where London ends,
   New towns have filled the fields of root
Where father and his business friends
   Drove in the Landaulette to shoot;

Tall concrete standards line the lane,
   Brick boxes glitter in the sun:
Far more would these have caused him pain
   Than my mishandling of a gun.

# N.W.5 & N.6

Red cliffs arise. And up them service lifts
Soar with the groceries to silver heights.
Lissenden Mansions. And my memory sifts
Lilies from lily-like electric lights
And Irish stew smells from the smell of prams
And roar of seas from roar of London trams.

Out of it all my memory carves the quiet
Of that dark privet hedge where pleasures breed,
There first, intent upon its leafy diet,
I watched the looping caterpillar feed
And saw it hanging in a gummy froth
Till, weeks on, from the chrysalis burst the moth.

I see black oak twigs outlined on the sky,
Red squirrels on the Burdett-Coutts estate.
I ask my nurse the question "Will I die?"
As bells from sad St. Anne's ring out so late,
"And if I do die, will I go to Heaven?"
Highgate at eventide. Nineteen-eleven.

"You will. I won't." From that cheap nursery-maid,
Sadist and puritan as now I see,
I first learned what it was to be afraid,
Forcibly fed when sprawled across her knee
Lock'd into cupboards, left alone all day,
"World without end." What fearsome words to pray.

"World without end." It was not what she'ld do
That frightened me so much as did her fear
And guilt at endlessness. I caught them too,
Hating to think of sphere succeeding sphere
Into eternity and God's dread will.
I caught her terror then. I have it still.

## Tregardock

A mist that from the moor arose
   In sea-fog wraps Port Isaac bay,
The moan of warning from Trevose
   Makes grimmer this October day.

Only the shore and cliffs are clear.
   Gigantic slithering shelves of slate
In waiting awfulness appear
   Like journalism full of hate.

On the steep path a bramble leaf
   Stands motionless and wet with dew,
The grass bends down, the bracken's brown,
   The grey-green gorse alone is new.

Cautious my sliding footsteps go
   To quarried rock and dripping cave;
The ocean, leaden-still below,
   Hardly has strength to lift a wave.

I watch it crisp into its height
   And flap exhausted on the beach,
The long surf menacing and white
   Hissing as far as it can reach.

The dunlin do not move, each bird
Is stationary on the sand
As if a spirit in it heard
The final end of sea and land.

And I on my volcano edge
Exposed to ridicule and hate
Still do not dare to leap the ledge
And smash to pieces on the slate.

## In Willesden Churchyard

Come walk with me, my love, to Neasden Lane.
The chemicals from various factories
Have bitten deep into the Portland stone
And streaked the white Carrara of the graves
Of many a Pooter and his Caroline,
Long laid to rest among these dripping trees;
And that small heap of fast-decaying flowers
Marks Lupin Pooter lately gathered in;
And this, my love, is Laura Seymour's grave –
'So long the loyal counsellor and friend'
Of that Charles Reade whose coffin lies with hers.
Was she his mistress? Did he visit her
When coming down from Oxford by the coach?
Alighting at the turnpike, did he walk
These elmy lanes of Middlesex and climb
A stile or two across the dairy farms
Over to Harlesden at the wicket gate?
Then the soft rigours of his Fellowship
Were tenderly relaxed. The sun would send
Last golden streaks of mild October light
On tarred and weather-boarded barn and shed.
Blue bonfire smoke would hang among the trees;
And in the little stucco hermitage
Did Laura gently stroke her lover's head?
And did her Charles look up into her eyes
For loyal counsel there? I do not know.

Doubtless some pedant for his Ph.D.
Has ascertained the facts, or I myself
Might find them in the public libraries.
I only know that as we see her grave
My flesh, to dissolution nearer now
Than yours, which is so milky white and soft,
Frightens me, though the Blessed Sacrament
Not ten yards off in Willesden parish church
Glows with the present immanence of God.

# DEATH

## Death in Leamington

She died in the upstairs bedroom
  By the light of the ev'ning star
That shone through the plate glass window
  From over Leamington Spa.

Beside her the lonely crochet
  Lay patiently and unstirred,
But the fingers that would have work'd it
  Were dead as the spoken word.

And Nurse came in with the tea-things
  Breast high 'mid the stands and chairs –
But Nurse was alone with her own little soul,
  And the things were alone with theirs.

She bolted the big round window,
  She let the blinds unroll,
She set a match to the mantle,
  She covered the fire with coal.

And "Tea!" she said in a tiny voice
  "Wake up! It's nearly *five*."
Oh! Chintzy, chintzy cheeriness,
  Half dead and half alive!

Do you know that the stucco is peeling?
  Do you know that the heart will stop?
From those yellow Italianate arches
  Do you hear the plaster drop?

Nurse looked at the silent bedstead,
At the gray, decaying face,
As the calm of a Leamington ev'ning
Drifted into the place.

She moved the table of bottles
Away from the bed to the wall;
And tiptoeing gently over the stairs
Turned down the gas in the hall.

## A Shropshire Lad

Captain Webb, the swimmer and a relation of Mary Webb by marriage, was born at Dawley in an industrial district in Salop.
*This should be recited with a Midland accent.*

The gas was on in the Institute,[1]
  The flare was up in the gym,
A man was running a mineral line,
  A lass was singing a hymn,
When Captain Webb the Dawley man,
  Captain Webb from Dawley,
Came swimming along the old canal
  That carried the bricks to Lawley.
    Swimming along –
    Swimming along –
    Swimming along from Severn,
And paying a call at Dawley Bank while swimming along to Heaven.

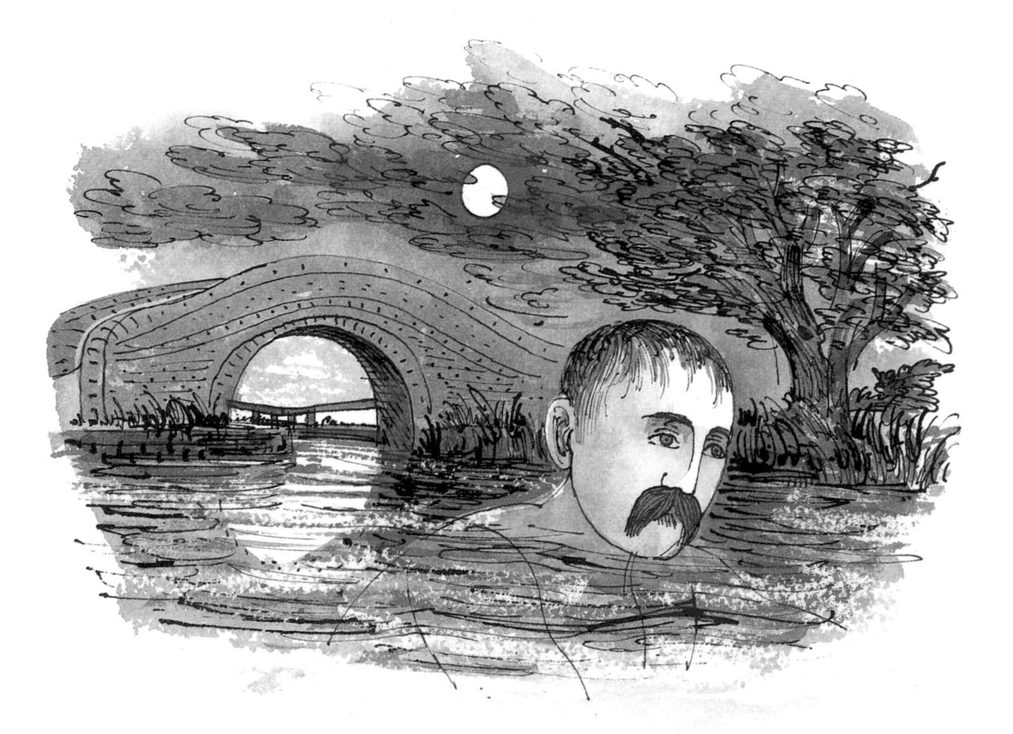

The sun shone low on the railway line
And over the bricks and stacks,
And in at the upstairs windows
Of the Dawley houses' backs,
When we saw the ghost of Captain Webb,
Webb in a water sheeting,
Come dripping along in a bathing dress
To the Saturday evening meeting.
Dripping along –
Dripping along –
To the Congregational Hall;
Dripping and still he rose over the sill and faded away in a wall.

There wasn't a man in Oakengates
That hadn't got hold of the tale,
And over the valley in Ironbridge,
And round by Coalbrookdale,
How Captain Webb the Dawley man,
Captain Webb from Dawley,
Rose rigid and dead from the old canal
That carries the bricks to Lawley.
Rigid and dead –
Rigid and dead –
To the Saturday congregation,
Paying a call at Dawley Bank on his way to his destination.

1 "The Institute was radiant with gas." Ch. XIX, *Boyhood*.
A novel in verse by Rev. E. E. Bradford, D.D.

## House of Rest

Now all the world she knew is dead
   In this small room she lives her days
The wash-hand stand and single bed
   Screened from the public gaze.

The horse-brass shines, the kettle sings,
   The cup of China tea
Is tasted among cared-for things
   Ranged round for me to see –

Lincoln, by Valentine and Co.,
   Now yellowish brown and stained,
But there some fifty years ago
   Her Harry was ordained;

Outside the Church at Woodhall Spa
 The smiling groom and bride,
And here's his old tobacco jar
 Dried lavender inside.

I do not like to ask if he
 Was "High" or "Low" or "Broad"
Lest such a question seem to be
 A mockery of Our Lord.

Her full grey eyes look far beyond
 The little room and me
To village church and village pond
 And ample rectory.

She sees her children each in place
  Eyes downcast as they wait,
She hears her Harry murmur Grace,
  Then heaps the porridge plate.

Aroused at seven, to bed by ten,
  They fully lived each day,
Dead sons, so motor-bike-mad then,
  And daughters far away.

Now when the bells for Eucharist
  Sound in the Market Square,
With sunshine struggling through the mist
  And Sunday in the air,

The veil between her and her dead
  Dissolves and shows them clear,
The Consecration Prayer is said
  And all of them are near

## Death of King George V

"New King arrives in his capital by air . . ." *Daily Newspaper*

Spirits of well-shot woodcock, partridge, snipe
　Flutter and bear him up the Norfolk sky:
In that red house in a red mahogany book-case
　The stamp collection waits with mounts long dry.

The big blue eyes are shut which saw wrong clothing
　And favourite fields and coverts from a horse;
Old men in country houses hear clocks ticking
　Over thick carpets with a deadened force;

Old men who never cheated, never doubted,
　Communicated monthly, sit and stare
At the new suburb stretched beyond the run-way
　Where a young man lands hatless from the air.

## Devonshire Street W.1

The heavy mahogany door with its wrought-iron screen
   Shuts. And the sound is rich, sympathetic, discreet.
The sun still shines on this eighteenth-century scene
   With Edwardian faience adornments – Devonshire Street.

No hope. And the X-ray photographs under his arm
   Confirm the message. His wife stands timidly by.
The opposite brick-built house looks lofty and calm
   Its chimneys steady against a mackerel sky.

No hope. And the iron nob of this palisade
   So cold to the touch, is luckier now than he
"Oh merciless, hurrying Londoners! Why was I made
   For the long and the painful deathbed coming to me?"

She puts her fingers in his as, loving and silly,
   At long-past Kensington dances she used to do
"It's cheaper to take the tube to Piccadilly
   And then we can catch a nineteen or a twenty-two."

## Old Friends

The sky widens to Cornwall. A sense of sea
   Hangs in the lichenous branches and still there's light.
The road from its tunnel of blackthorn rises free
         To a final height,

And over the west is glowing a mackerel sky
   Whose opal fleece has faded to purple pink.
In this hour of the late-lit, listening evening, why
         Do my spirits sink?

The tide is high and a sleepy Atlantic sends
   Exploring ripple on ripple down Polzeath shore,
And the gathering dark is full of the thought of friends
         I shall see no more.

Where is Anne Channel who loved this place the best,
   With her tense blue eyes and her shopping-bag falling apart,
And her racy gossip and nineteen-twenty zest,
         And warmth of heart?

Where's Roland, easing his most unwieldy car,
   With its load of golf-clubs, backwards into the lane?
Where's Kathleen Stokes with her Sealyhams? There's Doom Bar;
         Bray Hill shows plain;

For this is the turn, and the well-known trees draw near;
   On the road their pattern in moonlight fades and swells:
As the engine stops, from two miles off I hear
         St. Minver bells.

What a host of stars in a wideness still and deep:
   What a host of souls, as a motor-bike whines away
And the silver snake of the estuary curls to sleep
         In Daymer Bay.

Are they one with the Celtic saints and the years between?
   Can they see the moonlit pools where ribbonweed drifts?
As I reach our hill, I am part of a sea unseen –
         And oppression lifts.

## Monody on the Death of a Platonist Bank Clerk

This is the lamp where he first read Whitman
Out of the library large and free.
Every quarter the bus to Kirkstall
Stopped and waited, but on read he.

This was his room with books in plenty:
Dusty, now I have raised the blind –
Fenimore Cooper, Ballantyne, Henty,
Edward Carpenter wedged behind.

These are the walls adorned with portraits,
Camera studies and Kodak snaps;
'Camp at Pevensey' – 'Scouts at Cleethorpes' –
There he is with the lads and chaps.

This is the friend, the best and greatest,
Pure in his surplice, smiling, true –
The enlarged Photomaton – that's the latest,
Next to the coloured one 'August Blue'.

These are his pipes. Ah! how he loved them,
Puffed and petted them, after walks,
After tea and a frowst with crumpets,
Puffed the smoke into serious talks.

All the lot of them, how they came to him –
Tea and chinwag – gay young lives!
Somehow they were never the same to him
When they married and brought their wives.

# The Last Laugh

I made hay while the sun shone.
  My work sold.
Now, if the harvest is over
  And the world cold,
Give me the bonus of laughter
  As I lose hold.